MAGE of GOD
IN YOU

Kenneth Copeland

Harrison House
Tulsa, Oklahoma

The Image of God in You

ISBN 0-88114-789-3   KC-789-3   30-00

8th Printing

All scripture is from the *King James Version*
unless otherwise noted.

Published by Harrison House, Inc.
P. O. Box 35035
Tulsa, Oklahoma 74153

The Image of God in You

So you want to make some changes in your life. Maybe lose some weight. Or get your finances in shape. You're geared up, excited, ready to shake those habits that have been haunting you and step into God's best.

You make some resolutions. Turn over a new leaf....

Then, all too often, something strange begins to happen. Your determination wanes. And, as your new leaf grows, it begins to look alarmingly similar to your *old* leaf!

Suddenly you're back where you started. Nothing has changed and you begin to doubt that it ever will.

That's happened to us all more times than we'd like to admit. But you know what? If you're a born-again child of Almighty God, it doesn't have to happen to you again. God has given you the principle and the power to make permanent changes in your life and in your circumstances.

Once you learn how, you cannot only turn over a new leaf—you can grow yourself a whole new tree!

But first you have to understand an important principle, a principle that's been in action since the beginning. It's the principle of the "inner image."

God Himself gives us the first lesson about it in Genesis 1. There we can see Him using the principle of the inner image to create the Earth.

God didn't just come upon creation by accident and say, "Well, what do you know! There's light!" No,

He first had a desired result (an inner idea, or image, of what He wanted to create) and then said, "Light be!" and light was.

Now, God didn't have any problems making the changes He wanted to make, did He? He took the principle of the inner image, added faith and the power of His words, and *(pow!)* darkness was changed to light.

"But Brother Copeland," you say, "that was God. Surely you don't expect me to try to act like God!" I most certainly do. Ephesians 5:1 says, *"Therefore be imitators of God—copy Him and follow His example—as well-beloved children [imitate their father]"* (The Amplified Bible).

If we're going to imitate our Father, we're going to have to put the principle of the inner image to work too.

Let me warn you about something though. Don't waste your time sitting around trying to dream up a positive inner image all on your own. That's nothing more than positive thinking, and while it's better than negative thinking (or not thinking at all), it will eventually fall flat.

What you need to use as the basis for your inner image and for the words you speak is the Word of God. The Word has supernatural power. And if you fill that Word with faith and speak it out, it will work for you to change your life and circumstances as surely as it did for God Himself.

Think again about creation. God wanted light. So He said, *"Let there be light"* (Genesis 1:3). The words He spoke were directly related to His inner image. He used His words to get that image from the inside to the outside.

Words are powerful. They are containers that can carry faith and love, or they can carry fear and hate. Words are so important that they can determine our eternal destiny. Romans 10:9-10 says that if you confess the Lord Jesus and believe that God raised Him from the dead, you shall be saved. Proverbs 18:21 says that life and death are in the power of the tongue. And you are the one who will choose which of those you speak.

In fact, that is the part of you and me that is so like God. We have the unique privilege to choose and speak words.

Just think about the power you have to speak words! No other creature has the power you have. You may say, "Well, angels can speak." Yes, but they don't have the power to choose what they say. They say what they are told to say.

Satan once chose his own words, but it doomed him forever. He said, "I'll be like God and exalt my throne above the most high God." But he didn't have the right to choose those words.

Words can destroy—or they can create. They can take an inner image and project it to the outside world. Once you understand that, you're well on your way to putting the principle of the inner image to work in your life. But there's still one important question we haven't answered yet.

What do you do if your inner image is all wrong?

That's a problem that all of us face. You may be struggling to be thin while your inner image of yourself remains fat. You may be working to be a winner while seeing yourself as a loser. How do you change that?

With the Word of God and only with the Word of God!

You see, words not only release the creative force of faith, they also produce images. When you hear the word dog, the letters D-O-G don't run across your consciousness, do they? No, you immediately form a picture in your mind of a dog. You may even think of your dog. But if you heard big, black, mean dog, you would get a totally different picture in your mind. Words paint pictures in our minds.

That's why, in Joshua 1, God told Joshua to not let the book of the law (God's Word) depart out of his mouth. God told Joshua to meditate in it day and night. Why? *That you may observe and do according to all that is written in it; for then you shall make your way prosperous; and then you shall deal wisely and have good* success" (Joshua 1:8, *The Amplified Bible*). To *observe* means "to see." God was telling Joshua that if he would meditate on the Word day and night, he would get an image of that Word inside him. And Joshua *needed* that image. He was going to have to lead an entire nation and step into the shoes of a man who'd literally been with God Almighty.

Joshua couldn't afford to see himself as a loser or even as simply an ordinary man. He had to become what God intended for him to be by meditating the Word of God. And God promised him that the result would be wisdom, prosperity and good success. The Word of God would change what was happening on the inside AND the outside of him.

It's important to understand that we're not just talking about improving your self-image here. We're talking about getting that image to line up with the Word of God.

The Word of God. That's the key. So let's take a closer look at that Word.

John 1:1-4 tells us that *"In the beginning was the Word, and the Word was with God, and the Word was God. The same was in the beginning with God. All things were made by him; and without him was not any thing made that was made. In him was life; and the life was the light of men."*

If all things were made by Him and the Word is God, then I believe we have license to say that all things were made by the Word. Hebrews 11:3 says, *"Through faith we understand that the worlds were framed by the word of God, so that things which are seen were not made of things which do appear."* Everything that is, everything that has been and everything that ever will be was brought about either directly or indirectly by the Word of God.

If, as the writer of Hebrews says, the things we see were *not* made of things which do appear, what were they made of? Faith! Verse 1 says that *"faith is the substance of things hoped for, the evidence of things not seen."*

God's words are not empty like men's are. God's words are packed with faith. In fact, that faith is the energy that is in the Word that gives it the power to bring itself to pass.

In Isaiah 55:11, the Lord says, *"So shall my word be that goeth forth out of my mouth: it shall not return unto me void, but it shall accomplish that which I please, and it shall prosper in the thing whereto I sent it."* God's Word is a living thing. It has the

.nherent power to cause itself to come to pass. It is alive with God's own faith.

Just as God's faith energized His Words and caused what He spoke to come into being for Him, the faith He has given you, mixed with His Word, can create new realities in your life.

I've had some believers try to tell me that they just didn't have any faith—but I know that's not true, not if they've been born again. According to Romans 12:3, God has dealt to every man (and that's bound to include you) the *measure* of faith.

Now, by the power of the Holy Spirit, you have faith inside you as a born-again believer. So, when your inner image matches God's Word, then your faith can produce the end result that God desires for it to produce. In this way, you become a co-laborer with Him, bringing His will to pass on this Earth.

Stop and think about that a minute. Co-laborers with Almighty God! You need to realize that once you begin to put these principles and this power to work in your life, you're going to run into some heavy resistance from Satan. He's going to do everything he can to stop you because, as a co-laborer with God, you become his greatest enemy. And because he understands the power of the inner image, he's going to work hard to distort that image, to uproot the Word of God that's been planted inside you.

Jesus Himself warned us of his devilish tactics in the parable of the sower, Mark 4:14-20.

The sower soweth the word. And these are they by the way side, where the word is sown; but when they have heard, Satan cometh immediately, and taketh away the word that was sown in their hearts. And these are they likewise which are sown on stony ground; who, when they have heard the word, immediately receive it with gladness; And have no root in themselves, and so endure but for a time: afterward, when affliction or persecution ariseth for the word's sake, immediately they are offended. And these are they which are sown among thorns; such as hear the word, and the cares of this world, and the deceitfulness of riches, and the lusts of other things entering in, choke the word, and it

becometh unfruitful. And these are they which are sown on good ground; such as hear the word, and receive it, and bring forth fruit, some thirty-fold, some sixty, and some an hundred.

First of all, I want you to notice that the Word is the subject of this parable, not the ground in which the Word is sown. You'll notice that persecution and affliction arise *for the Word's sake*. Satan has to stop the Word from taking root in your heart. He has to stop you from cultivating an inner image of the Word. Once you have an inner image, nothing can stop you from receiving from God—you are fully persuaded that what God has promised, He is able also to perform. Satan must try to stop you before you become fully persuaded.

Remember, the Word has within itself the power to bring itself to pass. Once you get in agreement with the Word, Satan can't stop it from coming to pass in your life. It's the Word he's after, not just you! And he only has five things to use to steal the Word from you—persecution, affliction, the cares of this world, the deceitfulness of riches and the lusts of other things.

Satan uses these five things to try and get your mind off the Word and onto natural things. And there's only one way to overcome his methods. Follow the advice the Apostle Paul gives in 2 Corinthians 5:7 and *walk by faith, not by sight.* Even when your body says you are sick, you can believe that you are healed. How? By focusing your spiritual eyes on the Word of God that says, "By His stripes you were healed."

Just like Joshua, keep meditating on the Word of God day and night until it wells up as truth inside you and comes spilling out of your mouth in the form of faith-filled words!

Once you have the same image inside of you that is inside of God, then you can be confident that your body is going to change. It has no choice. It has to line up with God's Word.

"Look not at the things which are seen, but at the things which are not seen: for the things which are seen are temporal; but the things which are not seen are eternal" (2 Corinthians 4:18). Temporal things, like sickness and disease, are subject to change. The Word is eternal and not subject to change. An inner image of the Word of God spoken in faith will cause the natural (or temporal) to change. It will cause the natural to

change to match the image you have inside.

Visualize the Word as the paint and the Holy Spirit as the artist. As you read and meditate the Word of God, the Holy Spirit takes the Word and paints an accurate picture of God on the canvas of your heart. With that clear image on the inside of you, you release your faith, just as God did, and that which is in you becomes a reality on the outside. Your faith produces the end result God desires for it to produce.

God has given you everything you need—made you a spirit being, given you a mind and an imagination. He's given you the faith, and He's given you His Word with which to frame the accurate picture. He's also given you the Holy Spirit, the One Who is the power to bring the Word of God to pass in your life.

So get into that Word. Let it begin to shape the images within you. Then speak it out in power and in faith. You'll soon find you can make those long-awaited changes in yourself and in your circumstances. You'll not only be able to turn over a new leaf, you'll be able to grow a whole new tree! A tree of goodness and life. A tree that's bursting with the fruits of the Spirit. A tree that springs from the image of God in you!

Prayer for Salvation and Baptism in the Holy Spirit

Heavenly Father, I come to You in the Name of Jesus. Your Word says, *"Whosoever shall call on the name of the Lord shall be saved"* (Acts 2:21). I am calling on You. I pray and ask Jesus to come into my heart and be Lord over my life, according to Romans 10:9-10: *"If thou shalt confess with thy mouth the Lord Jesus, and shalt believe in thine heart that God hath raised him from the dead, thou shalt be saved. For with the heart man believeth unto righteousness; and with the mouth confession is made unto salvation."* I do that now. I confess that Jesus is Lord, and I believe in my heart that God raised Him from the dead.

I am now reborn! I am a Christian—a child of Almighty God! I am saved! You also said in Your Word, *"If ye then, being evil, know how to give good gifts unto your children: HOW MUCH MORE shall your heavenly Father give the Holy Spirit to them that ask him?"* (Luke 11:13). I'm also asking You to fill me with the Holy Spirit. Holy Spirit, rise up within me as I praise God. I fully expect to speak with other tongues as You give me utterance (Acts 2:4).

Begin to praise God for filling you with the Holy Spirit. Speak those words and syllables you receive—not in your own language, but the language given to you by the Holy Spirit. You have to use your own voice. God will not force you to speak. Worship and praise Him in your heavenly language—in other tongues.

Continue with the blessing God has given you and pray in tongues each day.

You are a born-again, Spirit-filled believer. You'll never be the same!

Find a good Word of God preaching church, and become a part of a church family who will love and care for you as you love and care for them.

We need to be hooked up to each other. It increases our strength in God. It's God's plan for us.

About the Author

For more than 32 years, Kenneth Copeland has led countless believers on a journey to maturity in the principles of faith, love, healing, prosperity, redemption and righteousness. Through the Believers Voice of Victory broadcast—one of the top five Neilsen-rated inspirational programs—and BVOV Magazine, he has brought revelation knowledge on the truths of God's Word. He has taught Christians everywhere that they can conquer the problems and challenges life brings through faith in God's Word.

Books Available from
Kenneth Copeland Ministries

by Kenneth Copeland

A Ceremony of Marriage
A Matter of Choice
Covenant of Blood
Faith and Patience—The Power Twins
Freedom From Fear
Giving and Receiving
Honor—Walking in Honesty, Truth and Integrity
How to Conquer Strife
How to Discipline Your Flesh
How to Receive Communion
Living at the End of Time—A Time of Supernatural Increase
Love Never Fails
Managing God's Mutual Funds
Now Are We in Christ Jesus
Our Covenant With God
Prayer—Your Foundation for Success
Prosperity: The Choice Is Yours
Rumors of War
Sensitivity of Heart
Six Steps to Excellence in Ministry
Sorrow Not! Winning Over Grief and Sorrow
The Decision Is Yours
The Force of Faith
The Force of Righteousness
The Image of God in You
The Laws of Prosperity
The Mercy of God
The Miraculous Realm of God's Love
The Outpouring of the Spirit—The Result of Prayer
The Power of the Tongue
The Power to Be Forever Free
The Troublemaker
The Winning Attitude
Turn Your Hurts Into Harvests
Welcome to the Family
You Are Healed!
Your Right-Standing With God

by Gloria Copeland

And Jesus Healed Them All
Are You Ready?
Build Your Financial Foundation
Build Yourself an Ark
Fight On!
God's Prescription for Divine Health
God's Success Formula
God's Will for You
God's Will for Your Healing
God's Will is Prosperity
God's Will Is the Holy Spirit
Harvest of Health
Hidden Treasures
Living Contact

No Deposit—No Return
Pleasing the Father
Pressing In—It's Worth It All
Shine On!
The Power to Live a New Life
The Unbeatable Spirit of Faith
* Walk in the Spirit
Walk With God
Well Worth the Wait

Books Co-Authored by Kenneth and Gloria Copeland

Family Promises
Healing Promises
Prosperity Promises
Protection Promises

From Faith to Faith—A Daily Guide to Victory
From Faith to Faith—A Perpetual Calendar

One Word From God Series
- One Word from God Can Change Your Destiny
- One Word from God Can Change Your Family
- One Word from God Can Change Your Finances
- One Word from God Can Change Your Formula for Success
- One Word from God Can Change Your Health
- One Word from God Can Change Your Nation
- One Word from God Can Change Your Prayer Life
- One Word from God Can Change Your Relationships

Over the Edge—A Youth Devotional
Over the Edge Xtreme Planner for Students—
   Designed for the School Year

Pursuit of His Presence—A Daily Devotional
Pursuit of His Presence—A Perpetual Calendar

Other Books Published by KCP
The First 30 Years—A Journey of Faith
   The story of the lives of Kenneth and Gloria Copeland
Real People. Real Needs. Real Victories.
   A book of testimonies to encourage your faith.

John G. Lake—His Life, His Sermons, His Boldness of Faith
The Holiest of All, by Andrew Murray
The New Testament in Modern Speech,
   by Richard Francis Weymouth

Products Designed for Today's Children and Youth
Baby Praise Board Book
Baby Praise Christmas Board Book
Noah's Ark Coloring Book
Shout! Super-Activity Book

Commander Kellie and the Superkids Adventure Novels
#1   Escape from Jungle Island
#2   In Pursuit of the Enemy
#3   Mysterious Presence, The
#4   Quest for the Second Half, The

SWORD Adventure Book

Available in Spanish

World Offices
of Kenneth Copeland Ministries

For more information and a free catalog, please write the office nearest you.

Kenneth Copeland Ministries
Fort Worth, Texas 76192-0001

Kenneth Copeland
Locked Bag 2600
Mansfield Delivery Centre
QUEENSLAND 4122
AUSTRALIA

Kenneth Copeland
Post Office Box 15
BATH
BA1 1GD
ENGLAND U.K.

Kenneth Copeland
Private Bag X 909
FONTAINEBLEAU 2032
REPUBLIC OF SOUTH AFRICA

Kenneth Copeland
Post Office Box 378
SURREY, BC V3T 5B6
CANADA

UKRAINE
L'VIV 290000
Post Office Box 84
Kenneth Copeland
L'VIV 290000
UKRAINE

Learn more about Kenneth Copeland Ministries
by visiting our website at:
www.kcm.org

WE'RE HERE FOR YOU!

Believer's Voice of Victory Television Broadcast

Join Kenneth and Gloria Copeland, and the *Believer's Voice of Victory* broadcasts Monday through Friday and on Sunday each week, and learn how faith in God's Word can take your life from ordinary to extraordinary. This teaching from God's Word is designed to get you where you want to be—*on top!*

You can catch the *Believer's Voice of Victory* broadcast on your local, cable or satellite channels.

*Check your local listings for times and stations in your area.

Believer's Voice of Victory Magazine

Enjoy inspired teaching and encouragement from Kenneth and Gloria Copeland and guest ministers each month in the *Believer's Voice of Victory* magazine. Also included are real-life testimonies of God's miraculous power and divine intervention into the lives of people just like you!

It's more than just a magazine—it's a ministry.

Shout! . . . The dynamic magazine for kids!

Shout! The Voice of Victory for Kids is a Bible-charged, action-packed, bimonthly magazine available FREE to kids everywhere! Featuring Wichita Slim and Commander Kellie and the Superkids, *Shout!* is filled with colorful adventure comics, challenging games and puzzles, exciting short stories, solve-it-yourself mysteries and much more!!

Stand up, sign up and get ready to *Shout!*

To receive a FREE subscription to *Believer's Voice of Victory,* or to give a child you know a FREE subscription to *Shout!,* write:

Kenneth Copeland Ministries
Fort Worth, Texas 76192-0001
or call:
1-800-600-7395
(9 a.m.-5 p.m. CT)
Or visit our website at:
www.kcm.org

If you are writing from outside the U.S., please contact the KCM office nearest you. Addresses for all Kenneth Copeland ministries offices are listed on the next

The Harrison House Vision

Proclaiming the truth and the power
Of the Gospel of Jesus Christ
With excellence;

Challenging Christians to
Live victoriously,
Grow spiritually,
Know God intimately.